"... I, on my side, require of every writer, first or last, a simple and sincere account of his own life, and not merely what he has heard of other men's lives; some such account as he would send to his kindred from a distant land...."

Henry David Thoreau

I Write My Own Epitaph

Clarence Jasper

FIRST PRINTING: SEPTEMBER 2010

WANDERING BROTHERS PUBLISHING, 419 PLATEAU DRIVE, FLORISSANT, CO 80816

ISBN: 0-9724917-6-7

PRINTED IN THE UNITED STATES OF AMERICA

Foreword

There are few moments in one's life to which one can say, "this was a cross-road; a time when had a right turn been made instead of a left the outcome of the journey would have been drastically different."

I was seventeen. I hadn't realized that I needed rescuing. I didn't know that I needed a mentor, role model, or father figure. Despite my lack of knowledge, despite the fact it would have been simpler to let a troubled young man find his own way, despite the fact that it was not his responsibility, my uncle Clarence took me into his home and under his wing.

Through his patience and example, I learned the power of stepping in to help even when no one expects it from you. Clarence's example of study to better one's self continues to inspire to this day. He took a would be high school dropout and provided the guidance that lead to my success as a working professional. Because of his quiet faith in me, I have attended college and have gone on to receive a number of professional certifications.

It was Clarence that secured my first two jobs. These opportunities were the foundation to my professional career as a senior manager.

Most importantly, I continually draw on Clarence's example as I now raise my son. As I encourage my son in his studies, as I teach him to respect others, to have pride in himself and his abilities, and faith that his family's support will be forever the bedrock of his future, I draw these inspirations from my uncle Clarence.

For his support when I least knew it was needed, and for the knowledge that even if that support is not needed today it still remains, I am forever grateful.

Cornell (Skip) Colbert
July, 2010

I Write My Own Epitaph

Clarence Jasper

Reflections

As I reflect upon my life, I am so grateful to GOD for my wife Blanche Colbert-Jasper, my son, Clarence II, my family and my friends. I am also grateful for my mountain top and valley experiences. During my mountain top experiences, I was on top of the world but it was in the valley that I grew – all of these factors made me the individual that I am today.

My life to the time of this writing has been so full that I'm driven to document the details that I can remember, so that all will know who Clarence Jasper was!

Beginnings

I was born December 20, 1939 in Cairo, Georgia, near the city of Tallahassee, Florida. I was delivered by a mid-wife.

My parents were Eva and Birdell Jasper. My father was also born in Cairo, and my mother was born in Whigham, Georgia.

I called my mom Eva, because that was her desire. She was of Blackfeet Indian descent. She was a beautiful woman, 5'5" tall, brown skinned with flowing black hair which reached down her back. Eva was mild mannered and easy going and very religious. She cared for her family like a hen cares for her chicks. The only way you knew when she was angry was when she batted her eyelashes rapidly, and at that point you knew you were going to be back-handed.

I was the only child breast fed by my mother which I attribute to my great health. My mother said I loved suckling so much she nicked name me "Titty." I am still called "Titty" today when I visit Belle Glade, Florida. I always told Eva that she was my woman and that we would always be together. My plan was never to get married, it would be just me and her, I loved her just that much.

Eva was a good housewife and spent the days cooking, cleaning, and tending to the family. In my growing up years there was never a day that I was not changed twice a day; once in the morning and again before my father came home from work.

I did all of Eva's running for her. One task I had was that, once a week, I would go to the chicken market to pick out a chicken for the family meal. At the chicken market the chicken would be killed and cleaned, the feet, eggs, beaks and other stuff were discarded in a barrel. I would go through the barrel to get chicken feet, eggs and other discards. With these, Eva would make a dish called Purlow: a mixture of chicken feet, onions, rice, peppers and chicken necks, with vegetables on the side or mixed in.

Eva's best friend was Carrie Nixon-Colbert, the mother of my wife-to-be, Blanche. Carrie was like a second mother to me; as was Blanche's father, Nathaniel, like a second father. Eva died of a heart attack during a church service.

****

I called my father "Daddy." He was the provider of the family. Being a country boy he loved game meat: rabbit, squirrel, possum, raccoon and any pork meat and their innards. Eva would always prepare these meals for him; she could "throw down" when it came to cooking. Because I didn't like this cuisine, I was labeled a "picky eater."

My father was extremely jealous of my mother. Daddy was 5'6" inches, had a nice physic and thought he was a lady's man. He had a drinking problem which fueled his jealousy, to the point that I felt that I had to protect my mother and sisters from his violence. In-spite-of this, I still wanted so much to please him.

When Daddy came home from work I would take off his shoes and bring him the "headline" from the news paper. I acquired my love for reading from doing this because daddy did it.

Daddy was asthmatic and because of this condition he was unable to do much more than work and come home. I often wondered how he survived living in the climate of Belle Glade and in-spite of this, to my knowledge, he never missed a day from work. Daddy died at the age of 56 from an asthma attack.

****

Robert Jasper, "Papa," my Daddy's father was 5'9" tall, a strapping and strong man, and a very determined farmer. He did a fine job managing his household. He and my grandmother lived in Cairo. Their house had no indoor plumbing, such a contrast from Belle Glade. Their water was drawn from a well. They cooked on a wood burning stove and a fireplace heated the house. And then, there was the infamous "outhouse."

I admired Papa and when we visited I would follow him like a shadow. He made my first wagon. What I fondly remember most about Papa was the day he had James, Erma and I gather pecans that had fallen from his tree into the neighbor's yard. While we were busy picking them up his neighbor came to the door with her shotgun and said, "Those are my pecans." Papa retaliated with his gun saying, "Those are my pecans!" Now mind you, the three of us were standing between two shotguns: Papa saying "go get my pecans" and the neighbor threatening to shoot us. Being more fearful of Papa, we continued gathering the pecans.

I loved breakfast with Papa; the Maxwell House coffee always smelled so good. Papa drank his coffee from his saucer. I always wanted to taste some of his coffee, but Papa would say, "Coffee will make you black;" to which I would reply, "Then I want to be just like you."

Legacy

Papa was a 33rd degree Mason, which is the highest degree one can receive in the Mason. He was very well respected by the community and the members of the Masonic lodge. Upon his death, Papa's body laid in state at the house where two Mason members would sit from dusk to dawn at the head and foot of his casket.   On the day of his funeral, the Masons bore his casket upon their shoulders and walked to the church, about one mile. This was their way of paying tribute to his position.

****

Annie Jasper, "Mama," my father's mother, was 5'5" a very fiery lady who never worked outside of the home. Mama was a terror in the daytime but in the evenings, after a dip of snuff, she'd chill out. From morning to sunset she was always doing something, washing, cooking, tending her garden and feeding her chicken. When we would visit in the summer in Cairo, we had nothing to do but play with our cousins or sleep in. But Mama was not tolerant of us sleeping in; she wanted us out of bed by 7:00 a.m. and her favorite saying was, "Get out of the bed so that I can air my bed clothing," and "don't let the sun burn a crust in your ass." In other words, if she had to get up early, the rest of the house had to get up!

So we always started the day early and then were off to our cousins' house. Erma would pair off with Virginia, I paired off with Claxton, James paired off with Vivian and Aramenta paired with Velma and Veronica.

We would spend the day playing hop-scotch, raiding fruit trees or going to the movies. At the segregated movie theatre the whites sat on the bottom level and the blacks in the balcony. We could buy from the same concession stand but the bathrooms were segregated and were marked "colored only." The most memorable summer time experience for me was when I went to Mr. Langston's house to raid his pear tree and I broke his mailbox. I blamed my cousin. Of course, I always denied my doing it. No one was ever punished. This was summer in the city!

****

John William, my mother's father left the family after his fifth child and contact with him was lost. I heard Eva say that he was a gambler. There's nothing much I can say about him.

****

Henrietta, my mother's mother, and Annie seemed to be cut from the same cloth. I called her "Mom." She was at least 5'11" tall, a very strict individual and very work oriented. She remarried to a man named Wiley Butler, a direct opposite of Mom. They lived in Whigham, Georgia – in the country – and owned 44 acres of farmland. The land contained pine trees, tobacco, peanuts and corn that Wiley farmed by himself. Wiley was an expert farmer and others would seek his advise regarding farming. On my first visit to the farm, I mistakenly mistook the tobacco plants for collard greens. My brother said, "Fool that's tobacco!" I had never seen a tobacco plant.

Henrietta died from a heart attack, fell into a fire and was burned.

When we visited the grandparents in Whigham (Wiley and Henrietta) I felt a sense of dread – pulling up to their house was like visiting the

Herman Munster's household. There was a large oak tree that covered the entire house: it was scary. Standing on the inside of the house you could look up and count the stars, but miraculously when it rained, it never rained inside. There was no electricity; kerosene lanterns were used for lighting. We used well water. The fireplace was used for heating and a wood burning stove for cooking.

Wiley was a jovial man. He could jump up in the air and click his heels three times before his feet would hit the ground. He was always being badgered by Henrietta.

One of the most amazing and funny experiences I had while visiting on the farm was witnessing my grandpa's mule everyday at noon. Without fail at noon each day the mule would cock his head up, give out a whinny, and head straight for the barn. It was time for lunch. Papa would be yelling "whoa mule!" But the one eyed mule did not care. It was lunch time.

When the mule died, we had a funeral for him. James was the preacher, Erma was the wailer, and I was the deacon. We blessed it and sent it on to "mule heaven."

Spontaneously Eva would have the urge to visit her mom in Whigham, and with my job having the flexibility that would allow me to take her, off we'd go to Georgia. I would drop Eva off in Whigham and then head to Cairo to rendezvous with my cousins and ole friend

Vivian. During one of our excursions in the country my cousin, Hoover Tolbert, and I came upon a mule being transferred from one pasture to another.

I saw this as an opportunity to converse with the mule, and _no_ I had not been drinking. I thought it would be a fun thing to do. I embraced the mule, and told it that I understood the pain and hardship it had to suffer working in the heat all day long, and then I planted a kiss on the mule.   I remembered working in the hot, sweltering sun from sun-up to sun down, and so I was compelled to show my love and respect for this animal!

When I was a Child

I was the sixth of nine children raised in a two parent home. As far as I can remember, we were never without shelter, food, or clothing.

My dad was also a farmer, so when I was nine months old, he gathered the family up and moved us to Belle Glade, Florida. Belle Glade is an agricultural town. The town was built in 1925. It is located near Lake Okeechobee, about fifty miles east of West Palm Beach, and sixty miles north of Miami, Florida. The area around Lake Okeechobee is fertile and farming is its primary industry. This is where all types of vegetables and sugar cane products are harvested.

Belle Glade is a small community of 30,000 people and because of its agricultural resources attracted migratory workers. Because of all the wayward migrants that came through Belle Glade, bringing with them their spiritual beliefs and cultures, Belle Glade was as decadent as Sodom and Gommorah. I remember many brilliant students that passed through Belle Glade, but many would only stay for a period, and leave because their families lived as nomads.
There were many strange residents of Belle Glade: Ma Rosa being one.

She was our neighbor and would throw her urine on the side walk to keep the spirits away. She was a Jamaican woman and very mean. She made coconut candy and sold it in the neighborhood: It was delicious!

Ma Rosa had her own church on her property which attracted many of the community children. Because of her culture she dealt in voodism. She had a spell that seemed to "draw" the children. The children could be seen dancing and prancing around during her ceremonies.

One Saturday, my brother Ralph went to one of the ceremonies, and came home "caught up in the spirit" saying, "Jesus, Jesus, Jesus, Jesus!" It took hours for Eva to get him calmed down. Eva said, "No more visiting Ma Rosa." After that no one ever talked about Ma Rosa nor was allowed to go back over to Ma Rosa.

****

Amy was my oldest sister. Amy was a very brilliant woman whose heart's desire was to be a nurse but there was no money to send her to college. This ultimately led to her resentment of the other children in the family, and ultimately led her into the streets of Belle Glade. Amy married Carlise Bennett and they had children: Curtis, Anthony, Christine and Larry (he died of AIDS). From this group of cousins came an abundance of second cousins.   Amy died of an overdose of medication.
My second oldest sister is Erma, my baby, and my ROCK! She's always

been there for me. In fact, Erma registered me in Elementary School. In my messes, Erma was always there to help! She financed my college tuition, and she encouraged me to strive to do my best, and improve my life. She was one of the people that insisted I leave Florida.

I was very comfortable in my environment but because of her insistence I finally left Florida en route to Pennsylvania. Erma married Walter Murph and had one child, Walter Jr., who lives with her in Dallas, Texas.

My oldest brother was Wardel; he died of an unknown disease at the age of 25. During this era VooDoo and witch craft were prevalent in our community. Up until the time of death Wardel was a healthy man.

Wardel was an immaculate dresser, very kind, caring and loving. I considered him a consummate brother. He was an avid baseball fan and a deacon at his church. My brother Wardel had to drive Ma Rosa everywhere, because she didn't drive, and Eva told Wardel that he had to drive her. It seemed Wardel and I were the only siblings that Eva always volunteered to chauffeur folks around. Wardel married Hattie Mae and had two sons, Monroe who died of Meningitis and Hilton who died from AIDS.

Next was my brother James; he was brilliant, lighted-skinned and highly favored. I wanted to be like James because he had so much going for himself. People admired him; he seemed to have it all. James was a devious person and very mean. James married Barbara Pollard but they had no children. He drowned in a lake in New York in his twenties.

Aramenta was next – my little sister. Aramenta was feisty and articulate. She had a call for the wild and it was my responsibility to pull her back in from that call as often as I could. She was a rebel! Aramenta married Samuel Bellamy.

She had a daughter, Lushawn and a son, Donny Edwards.

Ralph was the baby brother; and he was a brilliant man. During the Civil Rights period, he would talk the revolutionary talk; hence his nickname Rap Brown. When he saw wrong, he spoke to it, and I learned this from my baby brother. He married Glenda (Blanche's first cousin) and had one child: Shaka. Ralph got into a drinking contest and anesthetized his body. He never recovered.

My childhood, despite the racist attitude from the white society was full of play, love and joy.

Life around town

As a kid growing up in Belle Glade, I learned to have fun with what my surroundings provided. I swam in the "muddy pond" which was a little canal. My friends and I would chase the sugar cane train as it passed through en route to the Sugar Cane mill, knocking or pulling the sugar canes from the cars; and then we would sit by the tracks, and crack jokes, play the dozens, and eat sugar canes.

There was a soda factory "Grape Pop Soda" which made grape soda water and we were allowed to drink as much as we wanted compliments of the factory. It wasn't always fun and games for me though. At an early age, I learned to work in the field, picking beans, and pulling corn.

My best friend in life was Robert Kight – "Bobby Red." I met him through his Uncle who tried to pit us against each other and set us up with a boxing match. Both of us had a reputation of being good boxers. There was money wagered on the outcome, but instead of boxing Bobby Red and I snatched the money, and ran. We bought Lorna Doone cookies with the money. We vowed that we would always be friends and we remained so until his death in February, 2002. I spoke at his homegoing service. I dated Bobby Red's sister, Mattie Belle, for some time but when she became pregnant (not mine), while away at college I ended the relationship.

Whether or not I attended church was not an option; I was required to attend church. At the age of 12, I was baptized at First Baptist under the pastorate of the late James B. Adams. In the church, I participated in oratoricals and attended Boy Scouts.

I had a spiritual gift; I could dream dreams, speak things, and they would come to past. It had been prophesized to me that I would one day be a preacher. I didn't want to appear to be different; I wanted to be like the "boys" so I ran from the calling that was on my life.

The call of the wild ultimately led me into a backslidden state. I experienced every decadence that Belle Glade had to offer: gambling, drinking, whore mongering, hustling and was on the verge of pimping; but because I didn't want to contribute to that kind of influence on the young women in the community, I did not take that path.

I enjoyed dancing and had my own little crazy dance that I called the Funky Bootie; it's the same dance that, forty years later, became famous called "The Butt." My specialty was doing the one leg/knee split which I would proudly show off on the dance floor.

When I was in the sixth grade my teacher gave the class an assignment to go to businesses and individuals for donations. I don't remember the cause, but I took on the task, and came back with the most money: hundreds of dollars. I believe this helped build my character and created the "can do it" spirit that I grew up with.

I was the founder of the Student Council in Elementary School. One responsibility I had was to hand out punishment to students that received demerits; I was the judge. Punishment would be something like, washing the blackboards, cleaning the classrooms, and so on. These would be done after school and I was the overseer. When children would form groups to fight after school or get into mischief, and then see me coming they would shout, "Here comes the judge! Here comes the judge!" This was long before Flip Wilson made this expression famous. As I reflect back, this was my early training for the position I would hold in the Criminal Justice System: little did I know that the LORD was preparing me. It also showed how much trust and confidence my teachers and peers had in me.

Around the age of eight I began to realize the difference between the "haves" and the "have-nots." I began to understand how the system attempted to control black society and it was then that I learned the real meaning of being black.

I was required to attend an all black school. I drank from "Colored Only" water fountains. I had to go to all black theatres. I rode in the back of the bus and when approaching a white person I was required to lower my eyes, take off my cap if I was wearing one, and be humbled. Again, as I reflect back, this is the reason I do not wear a hat today.

In my teens, my brother-in-law to be was the manager of ACE Theatre, owned by a white man. My first job was selling popcorn at ten cents a bag and my pay was a half cent a bag. I worked my way up to the concession stand. I felt that because of the inequity of my pay versus what the Theatre brought in, I had a right to be fairly compensated for my work, so I found myself skimming a share of the daily intake off the top. I was making more money at the Theatre than my father was making as a foreman on a white man's plantation. I was never questioned about the ledgers coming up short each day.

At the age of 10, I had an interest in embalming. I spent a lot of time around the local funeral home. The funeral director of Taylor Funeral Home took me under his wings to give me the experience. I was a devilish child, and Sammy Dobart and Dennis Reddick, men in their thirties, were morticians. One day they locked me in the embalming room and sprayed the embalming fluid in the air. They also once picked me up and locked me in a casket. They were trying to get me out of their hair, but because I was so persistent they finally yielded, and began showing me how to embalm bodies. My first body was a one year old child. I hung around the funeral home for about five years. This might have been the start of my interest in chemistry.

It seemed that the greater the challenge the more determined I was to take the risk. Police would not allow children to go into the pool hall, but my brothers and I would always find a way to sneak into the local pool hall, and that's where I learned to play pool. If I must say so myself; I became a great pool player.

Although the schools were segregated, I had a successful high school career. I attended Lakeshore High School. It was there that I learned to play the French and Alto horn, participated in Student Government – serving as Vice President of Student Council and was voted "most likely to succeed in the field of chemistry." I also lettered in football and baseball. I was a jock, as I played football (running back and defensive back), and baseball (shortstop, second base and right field).

My homeroom teacher, math teacher, and science teacher had the most influence on me. My science teacher, Mr. Jefferson saw more in me than what I was producing and commented, "Are you just dumb or don't give a damn? Where are you?" That spurred me to excel in my scientific abilities where I had never been challenged that way before.

Going into my senior year, I only needed two credits to graduate: English and science; so the rest of the time I spent in masonry class where I learned the craft of laying brick and reading floor plans. I acquired enough skills to build a house.

Even though my father and grandfathers were farmers, I was determined that I was not going to be a farmer; I always envisioned myself sitting behind a desk with a secretary.

It was during my Junior High School years that Blanche sent a message by one of her friend's, Barbara Jean Smith, to me that she liked me. Blanche lived across the street from my house and we played together in the streets. I had no idea that she saw me as a boyfriend.

Blanche was fine; she had big bowed legs; she was very shapely and always well dressed. Blanche's father owned a beer and wine juke joint with a huge patio in the rear of the building where the young people would occasionally have a party. At least once a month, Blanche and I would slip out the back and do our courting. It got to the point that I wanted her to be my permanent girl, I was 16.

I approached her mother to ask if I could date her. Blanche's mother, being my mom's best friend – such good friends that they occasionally dressed alike – had no objections but referred me to her father for final approval. It was during this time that the proper way to date was for the young man to seek permission from the girl's parents. Upon approaching her father for his approval he had no objection. In fact, he said that he appreciated my courage, that I was the only boy to have the nerve to come to him to ask, instead of trying to "sneak around" with his daughter.

Everyone called Blanche's father Mr. Nat. I had no fear of approaching him even though he was known as a no nonsense guy. He took me under his wings; he saw something "special – different" in me. It might have been my energy, assertiveness, and, or my outgoingness, and craziness that I feel drew us together. I was readily accepted as their son.

Mr. Nat passed in 1958 while I was away at college. This news made me reach out to Blanche who was at home in the 12th grade. I sent her a letter telling her that she had to be the strong family member because she had the tenacity to carry the responsibility of the family; since her father was no longer there.

I attended Jackson State College, funded by my sister Erma and _faith_. During my first year of college, I was feeling my way and having fun being youthful. I played offensive half back and defensive positions

for the college football team.
During one practice my leg was
broken in a pile-up tackle. I heard
the coach say, "My best running
back; now he's broken his leg!" That
was the end of my sports career.

Shortly thereafter, I left school with
the encouragement of my white
doctor and my white English and
Theology professors.   They saw
something in me that did not match
up with the times of racial events
going on in Mississippi. Their
encouragement was for my own
good. So I crawled back home with
bags and baggage, back into my
mother's home, and began seeking
employment. Eva, Aramenta and
Ralph were living there. It was also
during this time that I came to the
realization that it was time that I
slowed down and commit to the one

lady in my life that I knew I wanted to spend the rest of my life with Blanche Colbert.

My first employment was that of an insurance agent at Afro American Life Insurance Company: an all black insurance company. It was a job that allowed me the freedom of movement while servicing a human need.

While employed, I bought my first two cars and paid to have a home built for Eva. Aramenta moved to Pennsylvania to live with Erma and to go to college. This left Ralph and me at home with Eva. It was during this time that I met the president of North American Sugar Corp. who, after learning about my background in chemistry, offered me the job that I accepted as the first black sugar analyst in an area sugar mill. Tiring of this job, and growing weary of the south and its racism, I set out to Philadelphia in 1966 in search of higher education and better employment.

I lived with my sister Erma in Parkwood Manor. Erma's husband was a policeman and she worked for Medical Records Child Guidance Clinic in Philadelphia: now Children Hospital.

Everyone encouraged me to get out of Belle Glade because they knew I could do much better than what that environment offered. This meant me having to leave Blanche and other close friends. Little did I know that plans for a better job and higher education would come much later; the LORD was preparing me for what was to be a monumental change. It wasn't so long after I had moved to Pennsylvania that Blanche came and we were married, and had our first and only child, Clarence.

My own family

Blanche and I moved into our first apartment at Fairdale Court at 11905 Academy Road which was an all white apartment building. We had to go to Human Relations in order to move in because they were not willing to rent to blacks. Racism in the north!?

Instead of a job with great opportunities, I went to many jobs from postal worker, to manager of several retail stores, to insurance agent to unemployment. The unemployment produced the lowest point in my life, my valley experience, fortunately, my wife had employment and by the grace of GOD we were able to overcome. It was during this low point that I secured a job with the Philadelphia Court of Common Pleas, Probation Department.

I started out as supervisor of the Alcohol Highway Safety Department of Probation and Parole which allowed me to have numerous travel opportunities. I had a $20,000.00 a year travel budget that allowed me to travel anywhere in the world to attend conferences for my enrichment. It was during my travel to New Orleans that I stayed in the French Quarters, right outside the 9th

Ward, the Ward that Hurricane Katrina devastated in 2009, that I met a woman on my way to Xavier University to exercise. I had asked this lady for directions to the University and somehow we began to talk politics and change. I was in my last semester at Lincoln University studying "change" and going through some "change" experiences on my job. She shared with me the problems they were having in the 9th Ward. In talking about changes she told me that I need to attend a meeting with her that was being held that evening in the 9th Ward and, before I knew it, I was on a bus with her going "only heaven knows where."

I attended the meeting and ended up giving a lecture to a crowd of between 50 – 100 people about change. I was scheduled to go back the next day. I remember being scared to death: afraid that I didn't know what the heck I was doing with all those folks. But due to my job commitment, I was unable to attend the meeting the next day. To this day, I don't know what the purpose of that experience was.

During my 27 year tenure with the criminal justice system, I received a Master of Human Services degree

from Lincoln University; I rose from probation officer to the position of Director and Coordinator of the Philadelphia County Drunk Driver program.

It was here that I was able to effect positive changes within a system that was known for its unfair practices towards blacks and minorities. I've worked along side judges, lawyers, state legislators and others to bring about change and implement laws and programs that are still invoked today.

Every morning before I reported to work I went to the Chapel of the Four Chaplains on Broad Street, next to the Masonic lodge and prayed and meditated for strength and direction for the day. At the time, I was a member of St. Matthews United Methodist Church in Trevose, Pennsylvania.

Although I knew about GOD, I became interested in Buddhism and wanted to experience what

Buddhism professed to offer spiritually. It was during this religious experimental stage that my family and I faced a danger that it was nothing but the grace and mercy of GOD that allowed us to survive. A friend who was involved with Buddhism introduced me to Buddhism. There is a chant that I had to learn that I was required to say throughout the day. One day my brother, wife, my son and me took a fishing trip in a boat on Lake Okeechobee, and it was during this fishing trip a storm came, and we found ourselves in grave danger.

The waves were tossing our little boat and water was spilling over into the boat. I sat at the stern to balance the boat while my wife and son sat at the other end. My son was crying from fear; my wife was screaming that she could not swim, and I was chanting, and lo and behold, we passed through the storm.

Now I won't say it was the chanting that saved us. In reflection, I whole-heartedly believe that the LORD's hand was on this experience to show me that He was in control, as He delivered my family from a sure death; for it proved itself over the next weeks as I experienced a spiritual revelation of how GOD works.

I built an altar in my home, a cardboard box called a "butsedan" which I mounted on the wall, and would chant the mantra morning, noon, and night. There is a wooden version of the box but Blanche would not allow me to purchase it.

Praise be to GOD, the butsedan would not stay on the wall. Everyday I came home from work, whether I nailed it up, or cemented it up, the butsedan was on the floor. After several attempts I got the message and said, "Okay LORD, I hear you," and I threw it all in the trash. This experience made me realize that there is only one path to Heaven and that is through Jesus Christ.

For a brief time period a friend of mine offered space at his bar and grill "John's Patio" for Blanche and me to operate our restaurant "CJ's Restaurant." We bottled and sold *CJ's Famous, Coming and Going Barbeque Sauce*: "you could taste it coming and feel it going." It was a money maker. We sold BBQ platters, ribs, chicken, potato salad, collard greens, but I soon realized that although the business had potential it was too much for the both of us; and coupled with the decadence of the "bar" scene, I decided to close the business.

Throughout my life I've met and impacted the lives of many people. My home, often times, would be full with men from the community that would come together and we would sit and talk on all subjects; I was deemed the subject matter expert. They were hungry for knowledge and I was eager to share. I would get calls all times of the day and night seeking answers. Because Daddy had instilled in me the value of reading, I became an avid reader, and my son, Clarence, acquired the same passion for reading.

I have been a mentor to a number of men. One such individual is, Darryl Grant, an entertainer on the Caribbean Cruise line. He always thanks me for being his mentor. I also was a mentor to Gregory Moore. He played for Teddy Pendergrass. My nephew, Skip, whom I raised, taking him under my wings as my very own, has always acknowledged my role in his life.

My Son
Clarence Jasper II

Clarence II, our only child, has been a true blessing to us. Clarence was and is a "daddy's boy." Most boys seem to lean towards their mothers but Clarence never showed partiality and has always enjoyed being with and around me.

Being an only child, Blanche and I agreed that he would have everything that he needed to be successful; hence, he went to the best schools from Kindergarden – College, and graduated in July, 1992 with a Bachelor Degree in Psychology from Morehouse.

Blanche was a school teacher and she ensured that Clarence was successful in all his academic studies. She was right there with him throughout his school years pushing him to excel! He was an outstanding athlete and received many awards for his achievements in sports.

Clarence attended the George's School in Newtown, Pennsylvania. George School is known as the best secondary preparatory school in the country. Blanche became a "fixture" there: ensuring that her child was receiving the best from both the faculty and his peers; ultimately both goals were attained.

During his senior year, Clarence spent more time at the school than at home because of his popularity. He would often bring many of his friends home for weekend and holiday visits. It was at George School that he met and befriended, Ennis Cosby: the son of Bill Cosby.

Ennis and Clarence played sports together: football, basketball and track.

At their football games Bill Cosby and I would often discuss our sons' schooling as we both wanted our sons to attend an all black college in the south. My desire was for Clarence to attend college for higher learning and not sports, which usurped Clarence going into professional sports.

Bill never said a word but he had taken a liking to Clarence, and as a result, on the following Christmas Eve, Bill called and told me that he was sending our son to Morehouse College: tuition free! What a Christmas present!

Ennis and Clarence remained friends until Ennis' untimely death in Los Angeles, California in 1997.

Clarence was interviewed by Time Magazine with regards to his relationship with Ennis; to see the article, do a web search for *clarence jasper/ he was my hero*.

Essence Magazine also interviewed Clarence.

We often vacationed in Florida and it was on one of our return trips back to Philadelphia that we decided to stop at Disney World. We spent two days there. The most memorable experience I had while there was when Clarence and I took the ride up Space Mountain. Blanche, of course, stayed on the ground. It was a very thrilling ride but I vowed that I would never go again.

My Wife
Blanche Colbert-Jasper

Blanche and I were married on August 12, 1966 in Philadelphia, Pennsylvania. The minister was Pastor Barnes.

Blanche and I always played together as children. It was not until Blanche made her interest in me known through her friend, Barbara Jean Smith, that our youthful friendship blossomed into deeper emotions.

Blanche has always been an orderly and clean person. She drove her father's automobiles and kept them spotless. Her obsession with order and cleanliness is apparent in her personal dress, in how she dressed Clarence II in his youth, and the way she checks me out thoroughly before I leave the house; and in our home Blanche feels that every item must be in its proper place. My office is an area that Blanche is determined to conform to her standard of order. In my office I have my own organization; if my papers are stacked up or scattered on my desk, it's my organization. But when Blanche comes through, everything is put in drawers and folders; and of course, I can not find anything when I go to look for it: that's my Blanche! Blanche is an excellent homemaker and a great cook.

Blanche is a very giving person to the church and individuals that have a legitimate need. Her love for GOD is unwavering and she readily shares her convictions to those she encounters.

Many of her co-workers, through her efforts, have attended our church and several have become members. Each morning before she leaves for work, we share a devotional period; I prepare her breakfast and see her to the door. I also watch her until she reaches and enters her car. If the LORD says so, I will continue doing this until she retires.

After 44 years of marriage (and I'm looking forward to many more), I still have a mighty job to perform within my family structure, and by the grace GOD I shall accomplish all that has been assigned to my hands, because I'm still standing.

Still Standing

I am now retired but I still commune with my special friend, Stanley Franklin, whom I met in the Probation and Parole department.

Stanley and I have a special bond, we both have our unique philosophical, psychological and political take on life and therefore we're bound into a special relationship. We spend countless hours talking about a full range of topics. And then of course there's my Christian brother and friend, Earnie Moore, whom I talk to almost daily. Both of us, being from the south, share common values and we have a love for life and having "boyish" fun. Stanley and Earnie are what I consider "true" friends.

I am now looking forward to what it is the Lord has for me to do. In the meantime, I'm a member of the Linconia Tabernacle Christian Center where Bishop Kenneth White is the Senior Pastor; it is here that I am the founder and coordinator of the Historical Ministry; work on the Financial Ministry; and serve as a Board Member and treasurer of the Linconia Community Center.

In 2007, Blanche and I were asked and we accepted to be the spiritual God-parents of our twin god-daughters Bryann and Brooklyn Jean-Gilles. I find my life filled with special individuals that are drawn to me and I consider them all to be blessings. As I move forward I still have time to travel, enjoy my family, go fishing, read, and just enjoy life. I'M STILL STANDING!

The Jasper Family Genealogy

Parents

Children

Tom Jasper
Father's Father, Father
(Great Grandfather)

Robert Jasper

Unknown
Father's Mother, Mother
(Great Grandmother)

Robert Jasper
Father's Father
(Grandfather)

Robert Jasper Jr., Don Cornelius Jasper, Birdell Jasper, Louvenia Clark, Anna Lou Jasper Copeland, Zettacar Jasper

Annie Brown Jasper
Father's Mother
(Grandmother)

Birdell Jasper
Father

Robert Jasper (Died at birth), Wardell Jasper, Amy Jewel Doward, Erma Louise Murph, James Edward Jasper, Clarence Anthony Jasper, Tina Jasper (Died at birth), Aramenta Louis Bellany, Ralph Emerson Jasper

Eva Jasper
Mother
Born 8/18/1912
Died 08/17/1983

Birdell / Eva's Grandchildren

Wardell Jasper

Monroe Jasper (Died at age of 10)
Olden Hilton Jasper
Born 08/28/1952
Died 08/28/1992

Amy Jewel

Larry Bennett
Born 2/23/1954
Died 01/27/1989
Curtis Bennett
Christine Bennett
Anthony Bennett

Erma Louise Murph

Walter Murph III

Clarence Anthony

Clarence II

Aramenta Bellany

Lushawn Jasper
Cornelius Jasper

Ralph Emerson

Ralph Jasper Jr.
Shaka Abdul Jasper

Birdell/Eva's Great Grandchildren

Olden Hilton Jasper

Lashaun Jasper
Quanda Jasper
NaTasha Jasper
Hattie Jasper
Yvonne Jasper
Hilton Rashaad Jasper
Hilton Jasper

Curtis Bennett

Sharon Bennett
Kevin Bennett
Shakira Bennett

Larry Bennett

Gregory Bennett
Drameko Bennett
Mewanda Gennett
Andreana Bennett
Markita Bennett

Anthony Bennett

Anthony Bennett Jr.
Carlisle Bennett
Leon Bennett
Blanche Bennett
Taquila Bennett

Great Grandchildren Con't

Chistine Bennett

Turshielda Hobbs
Sharon (Hobbs) Hill
Lakeecha Hobbs
Takiya Hobbs
Ammie Hobbs

Shaka Abdul Jasper

Destiny
Eva

Lushawn Jasper

Allen Jr.
Kashara
Anthony

Donny Edwards Bellamy

Nicolette
Dwayne
Donnie Jr.
Dashaun

Walter Murph III

Pamala
Terence
Jaquala
Aujoria
Lodoria

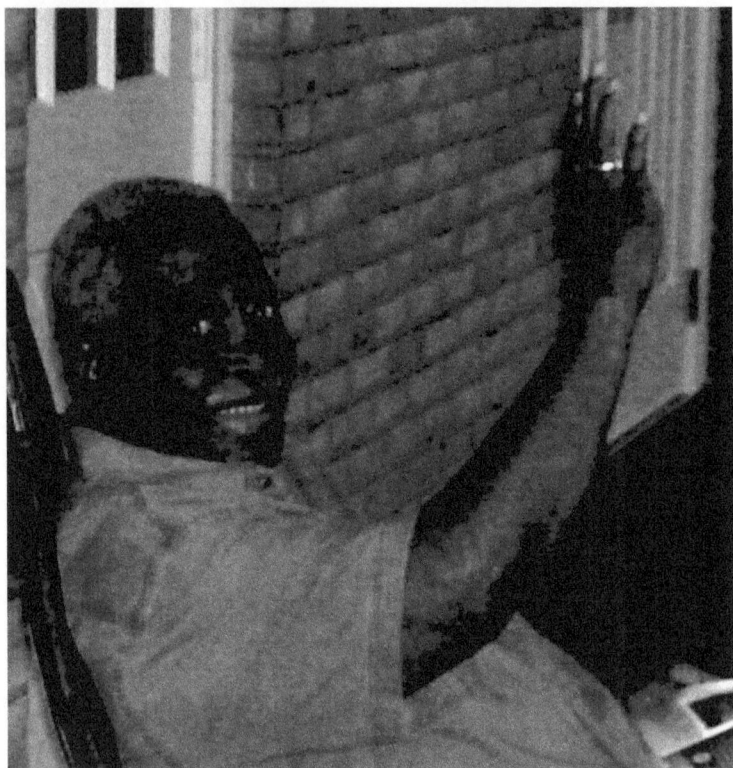